J MILLS

APPLIQUÉ

APPLIQUÉ

Jennifer Rollins

Bloomsbury Books
London

Published by Harlaxton Publishing Ltd
2 Avenue Road, Grantham, Lincolnshire, NG31 6TA, United Kingdom.
A Member of the Weldon International Group of Companies.

First published in 1992.

Publishing Manager: Robin Burgess
Project Coordinator: Mary Moody
Editor: Dulcie Andrews
Illustrator: Kathie Baxter Smith
Designed & produced for the publisher by Phillip Mathews Publishers
Produced in Hong Kong by Colocraft Ltd

This edition published in 1993 by
Bloomsbury Books
an imprint of
The Godfrey Cave Group
42 Bloomsbury Street, London. WC1B 3QJ
under license from Harlaxton Publishing Ltd.

British Library Cataloguing-in-Publication data.
A catalogue record for this book is available from the British Library.
Title: Country Crafts Series: Appliqué
ISBN:1 85471 136 9

CONTENTS

A simple appliqué using scrap fabrics.

INTRODUCTION

Through this Country Craft series, it is our hope that you will find satisfaction and enjoyment in learning a new skill. In this case, that of appliqué.

Appliqué comes from the French word *appliquer* meaning to lay on, and this is basically what appliqué is all about, the laying on and stitching together of different fabrics to achieve a decorative finish.

The historical development of appliqué has provided us with many different interpretations of the craft, from traditional North American patchwork appliqué to exciting contemporary art and attractive and unusual decoration for clothing. Household items such as tablecloths, napkins, cushions, lampshades, children's toys and wall hangings all lend themselves to this technique and you will probably be able to think of even more.

Appliqué lends itself particularly to curved shapes and this will enable you to create realistic designs with a degree of naturalism that would be difficult to achieve with the more stylised formalism of patchwork, a close relative of appliqué.

This book gives you all the basic techniques that you will need to carry out an appliqué project. It also includes a simple beginner's project that will give you some experience in those techniques, as well as the confidence to try something a little more ambitious the next time.

GETTING STARTED

SOME VERY EARLY examples of appliqué have been found in Coptic graves in Egypt and consisted of small embroidered panels depicting Bible stories which were appliquéd to linen garments. Other early examples include an Egyptian funeral canopy, made of animal hide and decorated with several applied designs.

A quilted and appliquéd carpet found in northern Mongolia of Chinese and Scythic influence and dating from around 1000 BC, combined applied animal motifs and decorative quilting with outlining in twisted cord.

The nomadic traders who roamed across Russia between 200 BC and AD 220 used appliqué on saddle bags, tents and carpets, whereas in China around the same period, applied motifs in silk were used on clothing.

The Crusades (1096-1271) marked a time of extensive travel between Europe and the Middle East. Knights returned from their travels laden with exotic embroideries, sumptuous woven fabrics and the fashion of protecting their armour from the sun with an overgarment appliquéd with an identifying emblem or shield. From this, heraldic appliqué developed and the period saw the birth of coats of arms and shields applied to all manner of banners and flags that were carried not only on Crusades but into battle as well.

The 13th century saw the rise of the great period of *opus anglicanum* (English work), which was justifiably famous throughout Europe for the quality of its embroidery, appliqué and cutwork.

Master craftsmen created decoration of incredible richness and luxury, enhanced with gold, pearls and precious stones. Many fine examples, seen mainly on ecclesiastical garments, still exist today.

While the quality of *opus anglicanum* declined after the Reformation, other branches of appliqué and embroidery were being developed, including raised work that incorporated padding under stitches and fabrics, and stumpwork, popular in the 17th century, where whole figures were padded and then applied to a background fabric. This technique was particularly popular for decorating caskets and boxes as well as for religious vestments where the figures were used to tell stories from the Bible.

Appliqué on quilts became popular during the 18th and 19th centuries, particularly in North America. The climate made warm bedcovers essential, so appliqué and patchwork, which traditionally use every last scrap of material, were attractive and economical solutions for the poor inhabitants. Every young girl was expected to make a 'baker's dozen' of quilts before her marriage and the appliquéd one, by virtue of the fact that it took longer to make and used more fabric, was usually the pride of her collection and kept for 'best'. For this reason, many

Opposite: A modern appliqué design, combining strong basic colours and geometric forms.

A traditional floral appliqué quilt.

appliquéd quilts from the 1800's still exist in good condition and we are able to trace their stylistic development.

The early designs were fashioned from squares of paper, folded into four or eight and then cut into sometimes very complex patterns. This shape was repeated a number of times over the quilt surface to form the overall design. The quilt was then quilted using shadow or outline quilting, where the line of stitching follows the shape of the appliqué.

Over time the use of appliqué was extended, and designs using both patchwork and appliqué in the same block became popular. The most common patterns incorporated patchwork baskets which overflowed with appliquéd fruits or flowers. The pattern was repeated, with small variations in contents of the baskets, over the quilt surface.

Appliqué reached the peak of its popularity in England and North America in the early 20th century. Intricate, complex designs were worked in many different colours over every imaginable item, not just bedcovers, but pillow slips, sheet borders, tablecloths, clothing, cushions and so on. Mass production also began to influence quilt-making and ready-cut templates for appliqué designs were readily available. Complete kits (including fabric) were introduced for an increasing range of well known patterns.

Contemporary appliqué takes many forms. Abstract designs, combinations of unusual fabrics or colours, imaginative use of beading or other non-fabric additions, make appliqué more than just a folk craft, but a real art form, limited only by the creativity of the appliqué artist. Wall hangings and soft sculptures, as well as more practical items such as clothing, quilts and cushions, are all within the scope of appliqué techniques.

As a hobby, appliqué is satisfying, challenging and creative. Once the basic techniques have been learned, the scope for creating beautiful individual pieces is limitless. Lovingly hand-crafted appliqué works become the heirlooms of the future and make very personal gifts for family and friends.

GLOSSARY

Appliqué The process of layering and sewing fabric shapes onto a fabric background to create a design.

Bias strips Strips of fabric cut on the bias which are used in appliqué to create narrow, curving lines, such as stems of flowers.

Blind hemstitch Otherwise known as slipstitch, this is an almost invisible method of attaching appliqué shapes by hand.

Fusible webbing A synthetic which, when heated with an iron, will melt. It is used to attach one piece of fabric to another instead of sewing.

Patchwork Scraps of coloured fabric, joined together often forming geometric, repetitive patterns.

Quilting A fine running stitch which is used to hold the layers of a quilt together in a decorative design.

Reverse appliqué A technique where layers of fabric are placed on top of each other and then shapes are cut out of the top layer to expose the fabric underneath.

Staystitching A fine line of stitching just inside the inner seamline of an appliqué piece. It acts as a guide when turning under the seam allowance.

Template A piece of paper, cardboard, plastic or metal in the intended shape of the appliqué. It is used to guide the marking of seamlines onto the fabric.

Vilene Bonded, non-woven interfacing, used to stabilise and stiffen loosely woven fabrics.

Oriental fabric combined with appliqué makes for original cushions.

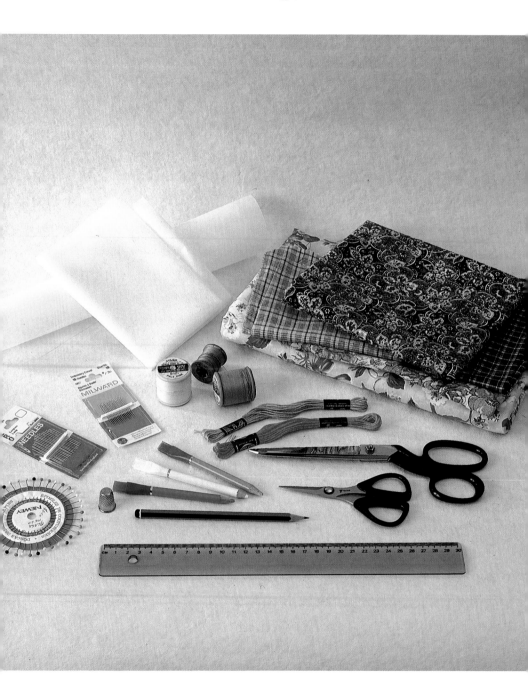

TOOLS AND MATERIALS

VERY FEW SPECIAL TOOLS or materials are required for appliqué since it is basically a sewing craft requiring only needle, thread and fabric. The choice of these basic items however will determine the appearance, as well as the durability of the finished work, so it is important to give some thought to what the work will be used for. Fine, gauzy fabrics and silk embroidery threads may look attractive, but will not last long if used on a cushion cover. These same elements could however, be used successfully on a wall hanging or as part of a decorative motif of a blouse that will be dry-cleaned.

THE BASICS

Fabrics Fabrics are obviously the most important element of the appliqué and should be chosen carefully with regard to pattern, colour and weight. It is not important to have large quantities of fabric, small scraps in a wide variety of patterns and colours will ensure visual interest and movement to your design. Spots, checks, plains, stripes and flowers can all be used to good effect, as can a variety of smooth and roughly textured fabrics. The background fabric should be sturdy enough to support the weight of the appliquéd fabrics that will be sewn on top. The best fabrics to use for hand-sewn appliqué, mainly for their ease of handling, are light and medium weight natural fabrics, such as cotton, linen and lawn. Polycotton mixes can also be used successfully, as can lightweight woollens. Very open weave, stretch or heavyweight fabrics are less suitable, either because they are difficult to fold at the seam allowances, or because they tend to stretch and therefore lose their shape as they are being sewn. Fabrics that crease easily are also harder to work with.

If you have decided to appliqué by machine, the choice of fabric open to you is much wider, from very fine silk organza, to velvets, denims, woollens, corduroy and even suede and leather.

Appliqué destined for clothing should be designed using fabrics with the same or similar weight as the clothing, and should have the same washing requirements. Remember to wash and iron all fabrics prior to use and do not use fabrics that you suspect will not be colourfast.

Vilene Bonded, non-woven interfacing such as vilene may be used to back fabrics that would otherwise be unsuitable for appliqué, since it will prevent fraying and also adds stability to stretch or loose-weave fabrics. It can also be used to prevent a darker background from showing through a lighter appliqué piece. Use only lightweight vilene since heavier grades will add too much stiffness to the finished work.

Thread Your choice of thread will be determined by the type of fabric you have used. Natural fabrics are best sewn with a

Opposite: Simple sewing tools and a variety of fabrics are the basic requirements of appliqué.

cotton or polycotton mix. If you intend to do some decorative stitching over the top of your appliqué, you may like to consider using embroidery threads, either perle cotton, stranded cotton or even crewel or Persian wool. Of these, stranded cotton is probably the most useful since it comes in a wide range of colours and can be divided for fine work.

Needles For fine hand-appliqué using cotton thread, 'sharps' are the best needles to use and are available in different grades depending on the weight of the fabric being sewn. If you are using embroidery thread, you will probably need to use crewel needles since they have a larger eye to accommodate the thicker thread. Heavyweight fabrics may be sewn with chenille needles which are thicker, longer and also have a larger eye. Special fabrics such as leather or suede will require leather needles. For machine sewing use a very fine, sharp needle.

Scissors Two pairs of sharp scissors are necessary, a large dressmaking pair for cutting out pieces of fabric and a smaller embroidery pair for fine trimming. A third pair for cutting out cardboard and paper shapes would be useful.

Thimbles Thimbles are useful for pushing the needle through heavyweight fabrics. Metal, plastic or leather thimbles are available.

Pins Long, sharp, glass or plastic headed pins will hold the appliqué pieces in place ready for stitching. More sturdy pins are required to pin the appliqué fabric to cardboard templates.

Pens Fabric markers or soft lead pencils may be used to mark the position of the appliqué piece on the background fabric or to draw the shape of the piece onto the appliqué fabric.

Fusible webbing If you do not wish to attach the appliqué by sewing, fusible webbing, available from fabric shops by the metre (yard), may be used instead.

Extras At the design stage, tracing paper, coloured pencils, paints or cardboards will help to plan the design of the appliqué work.

Opposite: Appliqué, reverse appliqué and machine embroidery on brightly coloured felts.

A traditional design looks effective when strong colours are used.

STARTING WORK

IT IS IMPORTANT to give a fair bit of thought to the planning and design stages of your appliqué project. Composition, layout, colour and texture are some of the aspects of the project which will need consideration if the completed work is to be a success. If you are just beginning to learn appliqué then a simple idea is best, working with only one or a few shapes until you have a good idea of the basic techniques. You will then be ready to tackle more ambitious projects. For the more advanced appliqué artist, complex shapes and dynamic compositions will offer exciting challenges from both the technical and artistic points of view.

COMPOSITION

The composition of the design will be influenced by the type of effect you wish to create. If, for example, you want to design a landscape scene, you will need to consider such aspects as proportion and harmony. The various elements in the scene should be related to each other in terms of size and the arrangement of the shapes should be orderly and consistent. If the scene is intended to be realistic then perspective, that is, the three dimensions of the design, is also important. If, on the other hand, you want to create a totally abstract design, other aspects of composition will come into play, such as emphasis (making one element into a principal feature) and rhythm (using patterns, repeating shapes and changing directions in the design).

COLOUR

As with any visual art form, colour is of primary importance to the overall look of an appliqué piece. Using our previous examples, a landscape scene would be best created using the soft natural colours and tones that one would expect to see in the real environment. Abstract designs on the other hand, allow you a much greater scope in terms of colour choice, as well as the way in which you blend those colours together.

An artist's colour wheel will give you a good idea about how colours can be combined successfully. The primary colours, red, yellow and blue, will dominate any design in which they are used because they are the purest and therefore the brightest colours.

Complementary colours are those which are found opposite each other on the wheel and which will vibrate strongly against each other, such as yellow and purple. Softer, more harmonious effects can be achieved by using colours found next to each other on the wheel, such as the gradations from blue to purple. Black, grey and white are considered neutral and will blend with any other colour.

The style of appliqué will also influence your colour choice. A 19th century appliqué design for a quilt will look more authentic if worked in colour combinations that one would expect to see from that period. A small child's appliquéd wall hanging of animals or the alphabet would best be made in bright, eye-catching colours, while an appliquéd cushion, designed to blend with your living-

*This appliquéd tablecloth
has been embellished
with embroidery.*

room furniture, needs to incorporate some of the colours already used in that room.

Do remember, however, that being too conservative and safe with colour can mean that the overall effect could be somewhat unexciting. Experimentation and a little daring can often create some stunning and unusual effects.

TEXTURE

Using different fabric weaves in the same appliqué will create interesting textural patterns that will give movement and depth to your design. Some fabrics, especially loose-weave or very thick materials, can be difficult to work with and the appliqué technique you choose, such as the use of vilene or whether to machine or hand-appliqué, will need to take this into consideration (see 'Techniques of the Craft'). In addition, different fabrics may have different washing requirements so, unless your appliqué will never need washing or you are prepared to consider dry-cleaning, keep ease of cleaning in mind when selecting your fabrics.

MAKING TEMPLATES

A template is simply a piece of cardboard, plastic, metal or paper cut into a shape that will then be used as a guide for cutting out the fabric shapes. You will need to have a template for each piece that makes up the appliqué project. If the same template piece is to be used many times, for example in a repeated design for a quilt, consider using stiff cardboard or even plastic to make the template. The template should be the same size as the completed shape; it should not include seam allowances.

Working from your original, full-scale design, use tracing paper to copy each shape in the design, numbering the design and the shapes as you go. The numbering helps if there are a number of small and difficult-to-identify pieces in your design. Cut out each tracing paper shape and attach them to stiffer paper or cardboard.

USING VILENE

Some appliqué artists use vilene instead of cardboard for creating templates. Follow the procedure for tracing shapes from your original design, but instead of using tracing paper, use lightweight vilene. Once traced, the vilene shapes are then cut out, ironed onto the fabric and used as templates. The use of vilene will also assist you in folding under seam allowances (see 'Techniques of the Craft').

When cutting out the shapes, keep in mind that machine-appliquéd pieces do not normally require the addition of seam allowances, while hand-appliquéd shapes do.

If there are overlapping shapes in the design, remember to draw each shape completely. The excess will be tucked out of sight later when you are making up the appliqué (see Fig. 1).

ENLARGING AND REDUCING DESIGNS

If you have found a design that you want to use but feel it is too large or small, it is possible to change the size by using a grid. Draw a grid over the original design. Then draw another grid the size you wish your design to be. Make sure that there are the same number of squares in both grids. If the design is complex and there are many squares in the grids, it may be helpful to number the squares. Find a square on the larger grid that corresponds to a square on the original. Mark the larger square at all the points where the design intersects with it. Mark all the larger squares in this way. Then

Fig. 1. Cutting overlapping shapes. The shaded areas are not seen in the completed appliqué but must be cut out as part of the template.

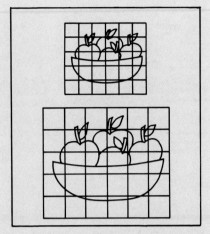

Fig. 2. Enlarging the design by using a grid.

join the marks with a line in the shape of the original design (see Fig. 2).

Many modern photocopiers also have an enlarging and reducing facility and for a small sum you can have your design copied accurately and quickly in the desired size.

PLANNING THE SEWING SEQUENCE

A design with many overlapping shapes will need to be carefully planned with regard to the order in which the shapes are to be sewn down onto the background fabric. This is particularly true of designs that rely on perspective and dimension for their effect.

Take the original design and number each shape so that shape number one will be sewn first, then shape number two and so on (see Fig. 3). Number the templates and fabric shapes in the same order. The actual appliquéing should follow the same number sequence so that all number one shapes are sewn first, then all number two shapes, etc.

A quicker sewing method, but one that is not as secure, involves placing all the shapes down on the fabric in the planned sequence, then sewing all the shapes down at once. This technique is acceptable if additional sewing is planned, such as quilting or embroidery, which will help stabilise the work.

Fig. 3. Numbering the appliqué sequence.
Shape No. 1 is laid down first,
then No. 2 and so on.

A traditional horn of plenty design is often
seen on antique appliqué quilts.

TECHNIQUES OF THE CRAFT

THERE ARE TWO MAIN APPLIQUÉ techniques, hand-appliqué and machine appliqué and while there are certain similarities between the two in terms of fabric preparation, the end results are vastly different. Whether to hand- or machine-appliqué will depend on a number of factors, including the intended function of the item, the type of fabric used and the style of the work. An appliqué design on a pair of children's jeans will be much more secure if machined, as will a very stiff fabric, while a quilt designed in an old-fashioned style would certainly look more authentic if hand-appliquéd.

HAND-APPLIQUÉ

Firstly you will need to cut out the fabric shapes and, when hand-appliquéing, a seam allowance is needed. Place the template face up on the right side of the fabric and mark the shape onto the fabric with a pencil or fabric marker. Remove the template, then following the original shape make another line about 3mm (1/8 inch) outside it. This will be the seam allowance (see Fig. 4). If you are using a very loosely woven fabric, make the seam allowance larger, about 5mm (1/4 inch). Sheer fabrics should have only a tiny seam allowance. At this point you could turn over the seam allowances and begin sewing; however two different techniques will make the actual appliquéing process a lot easier.

Opposite: Bold colours and a strong central design make for a striking wall hanging.

SEAM ALLOWANCE

The first technique which will assist you in accurately turning under the seam allowance involves the use of staystitching. After marking the shape and allowance onto the fabric, cut out the shape leaving ample fabric around the outer cutting line. Using your sewing machine, make a line of running stitches just a fraction outside the inner seamline, using a stitch length of around 1.8mm (1/16 inch) (see Fig. 5). Trim away the excess fabric and the shape is now ready

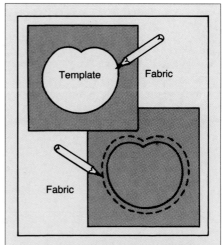

Fig. 4. Tracing the design onto the fabric. (a) First trace accurately around the template. (b) Remove template and draw a seam allowance about 3mm (1/8 inch) outside the original line.

27

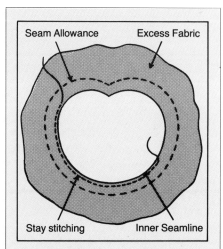

Fig. 5. Making a line of staystitching.
The staystitching is machined a fraction
outside the inner seamline.

Unusual framed appliqué designs create an
interesting corner in a bookcase.

A charming appliquéd posy of flowers.

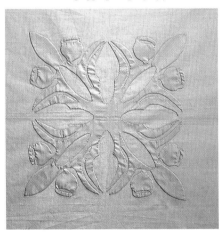

A piece of paper, folded into four with a design
cut into it, forms the basis of this appliqué

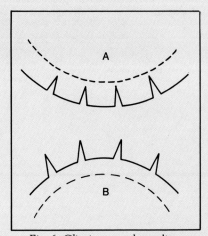

Fig. 6. Clipping curved seamlines.
(a) Inner curves and (b) outer curves.

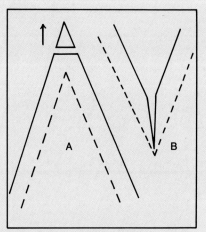

Fig. 7. Trimming corners. (a) Outside
corners and (b) inside corners.

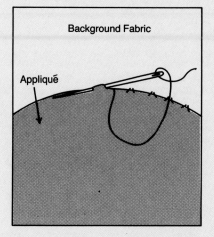

Fig. 8. Slip stitching. Bring the needle through
the folded edge of the seam allowance. Pick up
one or two threads from the background fabric,
then push the needle through the folded edge.
Slip the needle through the fold for about 3mm
(1/8 inch) and bring the needle out again.

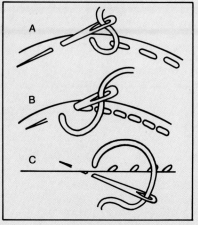

Fig. 9. Other appliqué stitches
(a) Running stitch. (b) Back stitch.
(c) Overcast stitch.

to appliqué.

The other technique makes use of vilene which, as mentioned before, can be used to stiffen loosely woven fabrics. If you have used vilene as an iron-on template, simply fold the seam allowance at the edge of the vilene. Stay stitching is not required with this technique.

Regardless of the technique you have used, folding the seam allowance under will be made easier if curved seams and corners are clipped or trimmed (see Figs. 6 and 7). The fabric will fold more smoothly and there will be less bulk underneath the shapes.

The folded seam allowance should then be tacked into place. As you gain experience in appliquéing, the tacking step may be omitted and the seam allowances simply rolled under the fabric. Regardless of whether you tack the seam allowance in place or not, make sure that the shape itself is securely pinned and then tacked to the background fabric with vertical tacking stitches.

HAND-APPLIQUÉ STITCHES

There are a number of different stitches to choose from depending on your patience and expertise and the effect you wish to create. The most common hand-appliqué stitch is a fine slip stitch, otherwise known as blind hemstitch. It is almost invisible if carefully worked and will hold the shape securely (see Fig. 8). Overcast stitch is slightly less time consuming, but care should be taken to make the stitches as small as possible. For these stitches, use a matching thread. Running stitch will hold the shape securely, as will back stitch, but these stitches are not invisible and in fact are often used as a decorative feature. The choice of matching or contrasting thread is up to you (see Fig. 9).

Corners and very deep curves have a ten-

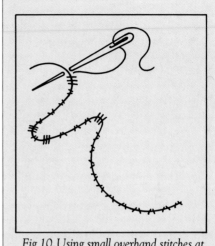

Fig 10. Using small overhand stitches at deep curves and corners prevents fraying.

dency to fray and therefore simple overcast stitches should be used to strengthen the fabric at these points (see Fig. 10).

MACHINE-APPLIQUÉ

When cutting out shapes to be machine-appliquéd, keep in mind whether the shapes overlap or whether one shape abuts another. Overlapping shapes require that both shapes be drawn and cut out as two complete shapes, while abutting shapes require one of the shapes to be cut with a seam allowance at the point where the two shapes meet (see Fig. 11). Shapes that sit directly on top of each other or that have no contact with other shapes should be cut without a seam allowance.

The exception to the seam allowance rule will depend on the type of machine stitch you choose, either straight stitch or zigzag stitch. **Straight stitch method** With this technique,

31

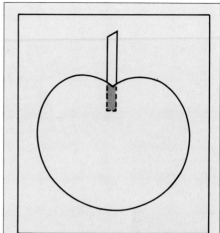

Fig. 11. Add a seam allowance
(shaded area) for shapes that abut one
another. The seam is tucked underneath
the larger shape and will not be seen.

the appliqué shape is treated as though it was
to be hand-appliquéd with seam allowances
and stay stitching, the only difference being
that instead of hand-sewing the appliqué
onto the background fabric, a straight stitch
on the machine is used.

Zigzag stitch method This technique is by far
the quickest and uses only machine sewing
with no seam allowance. Cut out the shape
with a generous border of fabric around it.
Machine straight stitch the shape onto the
background fabric around the seam line and
then trim the fabric to within a fraction of the
stitching. Finally, zigzag around the shape
over both the raw edges and the straight
stitching line.

A floral chintz makes an instant appliqué design.

This simple wreath would look attractive as a cushion cover.

Generally speaking, the zigzag stitch should be made with the machine on a narrow setting with a short stitch length. Very narrow stitching will give the effect of satin stitch, but this can cause bunching on certain fabrics. When using machine satin stitch, have the bobbin tension somewhat lighter than usual to create a well rounded, raised effect to the stitch. Textured fabrics are better sewn with a wider zigzag stitch, although decorative effects can be created with the machine on different settings.

With machine stitching, curves and corners can be a little difficult and the stitch length may need to be adjusted periodically as you sew, to accommodate tricky angles and curves (see Figs. 12 and 13). Occasionally fabric puckering can be a problem, especially on curved seams. Try slipping a piece of paper from a magazine between the background and the shape as you machine-sew. The paper

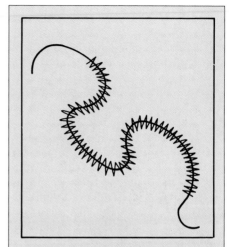

Fig. 13. Zigzagging along tight curves. You will need to constantly reposition the needle, at the same time pivoting the fabric to zigzag around the curve.

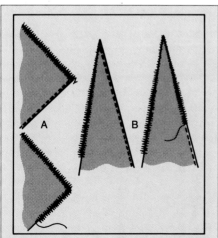

Fig. 12. Zigzagging along (a) right angled corners and (b) sharp angled corners

can be ripped away after you have finished the seam.

Vilene method If you have used iron-on vilene, you may zigzag directly onto the fabric, since the vilene will help to prevent fraying. You will, however, still need to tack the shape onto the background fabric. Tack close to the edge of the shape in the same colour thread as the shape and the zigzagging will cover the tacking.

STITCH-FREE APPLIQUÉ

This can be achieved by using fusible webbing between the background and appliqué shapes. When heated with an iron, the webbing melts and sticks the two fabrics together. It is only suitable for fabrics that can tolerate a very hot iron.

SPECIAL TIPS FOR DIFFICULT SHAPES

Bias strips Made either from purchased bias binding or from a piece of fabric at home, bias strips are very useful when you want to create outlines, stems on flowers or any narrow shape.

They can be positioned into gentle curves much more easily than a long narrow appliqué piece that is not cut on the bias. When appliquéing bias strips, sew the inner curve first and then ease the outer curve into the correct position by stretching the strip gently.

Circles Cut a piece of cardboard the size you want the finished circle to be. Cut the fabric with a 5mm (1/4 inch) seam allowance then sew a line of running stitches about 3mm (1/8 inch) from the edge. Place the cardboard over the fabric circle then draw up the running stitch, gather the fabric around the cardboard as you go. Iron in place, trim away the seam allowance, then remove the cardboard and you have a perfect circle (see Fig. 14).

REVERSE APPLIQUÉ

If one shape is completely surrounded by another, reverse appliqué can be used instead of normal appliqué. Cut a hole in the outside appliqué shape leaving 3mm (1/8 inch) seam allowance, more if the fabric is loosely woven. Cut the inside shape with a large seam allowance and place it behind the hole. Nick the curves and fold the seam allowance under, tacking in place as you go. Appliqué the top layer of fabric to the layer below (see Fig. 15).

Opposite page: A simple appliqué using scrap fabrics.

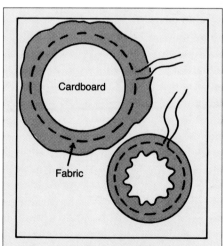

Fig. 14. *Making an appliqué circle. When stitching is pulled taut, the fabric is shaped around the cardboard circle.*

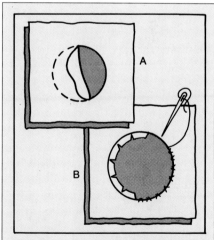

Fig. 15. *Reverse appliqué. In (a) the top layer is being cut out in a circle shape to reveal the fabric below. In (b) the top fabric is tucked under and appliquéd to the fabric layer below.*

*Quilting has been used o this
wall hanging to give added
depth to the appliqué pattern.*

An appliqué quilt incorporating a traditional floral motif and an unusual quilting technique.

FINISHING TECHNIQUES

THERE ARE A MYRIAD of decorative touches that can be added to a piece of appliqué, from beading and embroidery to fabric paint, quilting and sequins. Some of the techniques may also have a practical purpose. Quilting for example, will help stabilise and secure an appliqué if it has not been sewn piece by piece. Embroidery will also add strength to an appliqué and may provide the fine detail, such as the little eye of a bird, that would be difficult to execute in appliqué.

Other techniques are purely decorative and can be used to give added colour, sparkle or vibrancy to the work.

EMBROIDERY

This is the most popular decoration found on appliqué, probably because there are so many embroidery stitches from which to choose. In addition, the range of thread types and colours, from pretty pastel silks to the new metallic synthetic threads, means there is almost unlimited scope when it comes to adding the finishing touches.

Embroidery stitches may be used to secure the appliqué shape to the background fabric instead of machining or hand-slip stitching. In this case, blanket, satin, cross, feather or chain stitch would be suitable, since they are all closely worked and would therefore hold the appliqué securely in place. Additional details could be made using French knots, bullion knots, leaf stitch or stem stitch, to name just a few (see Fig. 16). An Embroidery guide will provide you with literally hundreds of different stitches suitable for your particular project.

BEADING AND SEQUINS

Specialist needlework and craft shops will be able to provide you with a vast selection of beads from tiny pearl-like beads, to chunky wooden balls and sparkling, multi-coloured sequins. If you decide to use beading as a decorative element, it will be necessary to invest in some special beading needles, which are very long and thin with tiny eyes. Beads can be used singly, dangled in groups or couched in curved or straight lines. Keep in mind that beading can make the item difficult to launder.

QUILTING

The quilting stitch is simply a fine running stitch and is used to outline or highlight elements of the appliqué design. It is particularly suited to patchwork appliqué and if you are using quilting with this type of appliqué, you will need to add a layer of batting and a piece of backing fabric to the appliqué and quilt through all three layers. Use a short needle called a 'between' to achieve small, even quilting stitches.

Note the strong linear design element in the flower stems which mirrors the shape of the harp.

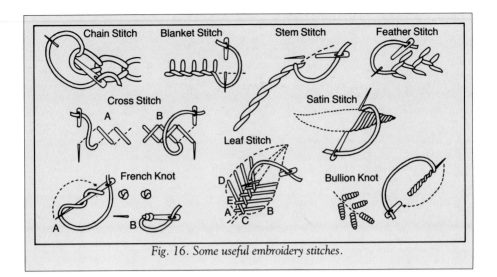

Fig. 16. Some useful embroidery stitches.

FABRIC PAINT

There are many different fabric paints on the market; some give a flat finish while others create a raised effect. There is even a fabric paint that acts like a glue and can therefore take the place of machine or hand appliqué. Enquire at your craft shop for these specialist paints and always follow the manufacturer's instructions to ensure washability.

STUFFING

To create a raised effect and to add body and depth, it is possible to stuff an appliqué shape. When sewing the appliqué to the background fabric, leave a small section unsewn. Using polyester batting or other suitable material and a knitting needle or orange stick, push the stuffing in behind the appliqué shape and then sew up the hole (see Fig. 17). Be careful not to overstuff a shape as this can cause distortion of the fabric.

Fig. 17. Stuffing an appliqué shape.

BEGINNER'S PROJECT

THIS BEGINNER'S PROJECT, an attractive wall hanging for a child's bedroom, is based on a very popular traditional design. While the design is quite simple, it will give you some useful practice in sewing those tricky curves. The work can also be adapted in a number of ways, depending on your creativity and sewing skill. For example, instead of using ribbon to create the balloon's string, you could consider a decorative embroidery stitch, such as chain or stem stitch. The balloon itself could be stuffed to give a three-dimensional effect, or a child's name could be embroidered in the background to give the design a more personal touch.

The design is also suitable to be used as a repeating design for curtains, as a cushion cover or, reduced in size, as a decorative motif for a girl's dress. The colours used in the design are very much a matter of personal taste. Creams, dark reds and muted blues have been used to give a traditional country feel to the wall hanging but you may prefer to use bright, primary colours, or whatever tones will match your decor.

See Beginner's Project worksheet overleaf.

Opposite: A traditional appliqué design used here as a wall hanging for a child's room.

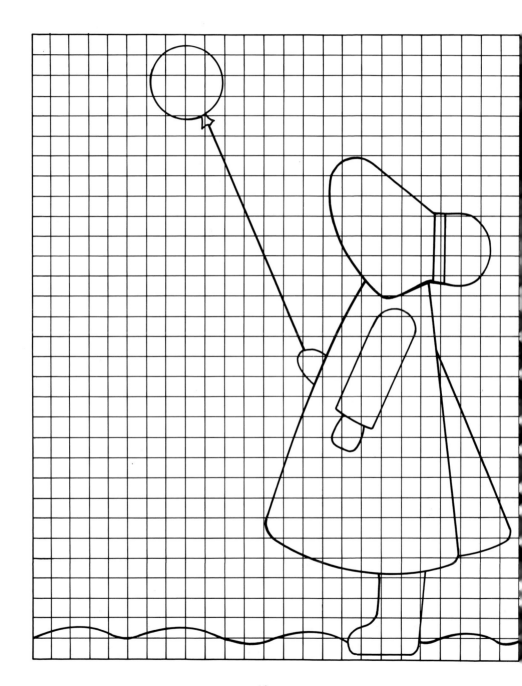

BEGINER'S PROJECT WORK SHEET

MATERIALS

For a finished wall hanging 28cm x 45cm (11 x 18 inches) you will need:

- 36cm (14 inches) calico
      (or other background fabric)
- Small pieces of coloured cotton fabric
- Matching thread for sewing
- Lengths of ribbon for the balloon string and bonnet contrast
- Dowel and cord for hanging the design
- Paper or cardboard for templates

METHOD

Step One

Wash and iron all the fabrics. Make paper or cardboard templates for each pattern piece from the design (see Fig. 1).

Place the templates on the fabric and mark the inner and outer seamlines as shown in 'Techniques of the Craft', remembering to include seam allowances for the parts of the design that will be covered by other parts, and then cut out the fabric shapes.

Step Two

The shapes may then be appliquéd in place according to one of the methods outlined in 'Techniques of the Craft'. For a traditional design such as this, it is recommended that hand-appliqué be used but if you are in a hurry, or if you intend to repeat the design a number of times such as on curtains or a quilt, it is possible to machine-appliqué instead. In this case, seam allowances are not necessary except for those sections where shapes overlap.

Step Three

The recommended sewing sequence is as follows. Firstly sew the left-hand mitten and sleeve to the apron and the ribbon contrast to the bonnet. Then appliqué the ground, the boot, the right-hand mitten, the back of the dress, the apron, the bonnet, the balloon string and finally the balloon.

Step Four

Machine-stitch the side and bottom edges of the hanging. Turn over and machine the top edge to form a pocket through which to pass the dowelling. Attach the cord to each end of the dowelling and your first appliqué project is ready to hang.

Opposite: Each square of the graph represents 1cm (1/2 inch).

INDEX